AMERICA'S SUPERCAR

JEFFREY HOFFMAN

JULIAN MESSNER • NEW YORK

JEM

A JEM BOOK

Published by Julian Messner, A Division of
Simon & Schuster, Inc.
Simon & Schuster Building,
1230 Avenue of the Americas,
New York, New York 10020.
JULIAN MESSNER and colophon are trademarks of
Simon & Schuster, Inc.

Manufactured in the United States of America

Design by John Treworgy
Edited by Jane Hyman, M.Ed.

10 9 8 7 6 5 4 3 2 1

Library of Congress Cataloging in Publication Data.

Hoffman, Jeffrey
The Corvette: America's Supercar
"A Jem Book"
Includes index.
1. Corvette automobile — History. I. Title.
TL215.C6H64 1984 629.2'222 84-534
ISBN 0-671-43485-3

CONTENTS

This one is for Jonathan.

Special thanks to
Mr. Harry Turton of
General Motors "World of Motion"
and Iris Rosoff and
D.J. Fuller for their kindness

CHAPTER 1

THE STUFF OF DREAMS

In 1952 a new star was born. This road and track star was the Corvette. It was the first of the dream cars to come true. Harley Earl was to play a large role in its birth. He was a car maker who knew youth. He knew their dreams, and he knew cars. In 1952 young people dreamed of a car with two seats. They dreamed of an open-air car with speed. They wanted a car all their own.

It was good, too, that at least one more General Motors' man thought the same way. His name was Ed Cole. He knew about cars. He knew about dream cars that young people would love. He went to see all the road and track shows. He went to race tracks like Watkins Glen and LeMans. He worked with the big cars at G.M. He was soon on the Vette team. The new car was on the road to fame.

The Corvette was first introduced at the Motorama in 1952.

The first Vettes were top secret. They were built in a small room at the G.M. plant. There, no one could steal the design. They were kept out of the way. Even at G.M. someone could say no to the birth of a dream.

Earl's aim was to make a car a lot of people could own. He wanted an American-built car that was fast and cheap. He dreamed of a car that would beat the world class cars in a race. He thought, too, of a car most of us could buy.

To make such a car, he would use stock parts from new Chevys. A stock frame would be used, too. The story of the first try at a Vette would make a good book. But soon Earl had to ask Bob McLean to make a brand new car from scratch. The real race was on. A great car would soon be on the road.

Most U.S. car designs start from the dashboard. Then they work to the front or back to the wheels. Bob began at the rear end. He drew the car from the back to the front. Other designers laughed at him. Bob stuck to his guns. Earl saw the new way. "Why did you do it like that?" he asked. Bob told him, "That's how they do it in Europe." Bob's new way put the engine in a little lower in the car. It was farther to the rear. This meant that the Vette would not be cheap to make. It would need a frame of its own. Yet the Corvette was at least to be tried. It would be a fine car. It would be fast. It would be fair in price. At least Earl hoped it would be.

The next task was to make a Vette frame. It had to move well. It had to use stock parts. It

The Vette was designed from the back to the front.

had to be smooth on the road and it had to be done in six months! As Maurice Olley said, "There was not much time." But he got the job done. It took only ten days!

The Corvette was on its way. Brakes were designed to work with the new style. Most of the car's weight was in the front. The old way was to put most of the weight in the rear. The car's center was down, too. The brakes came from the old line cars. Their new size was made perfect up to one inch. The old way made brakes that were less precise. This new way made the car stop very quickly.

The 1953 Corvette had a fiberglass body.

The Vette had many firsts. It had aluminum pistons. It had a lot of power. It had duel exhausts. All of this made the new Vette great. Track fans loved it from the start. Some fans did not like the new power glide gearbox. They wanted a four-speed shift, "four on the floor." The men who made the Vette said no. The car was built for the future. The fans would just have to accept it, and they did!

The car's most important first was its body. It was made of fiberglass. By the end of 1953, the Vette was born. Three hundred were made and all of them were sold. In 1954 ten times more were made. There were 3000 new cars. All were sold. The Vette was a winner for sure.

The next year bad news came like a flat tire. The sales began to slow down. No one knew exactly why. But, one reason may have been a roof leak. The Vette was to fail that year. Only 700 were made, yet it was not to die. The people who made the Vette had hope. They loved the new car. They felt it was the best road car of its kind. They would not give up!

Soon the Vette fans came back. The Corvette was their dream car. They would not let it down. If fans wanted Vettes, then Vettes would have to be made. They had to be made in great amounts, thousands of them. There were glass bodies. There were frames. There were gearboxes. There were small bolts and nuts. There were wheels. All of these parts had to be put together. It had to happen quickly. It had to be well done, and it had to be cheap. The Vette team and other company people had to meet. They had to talk about how this job would be done!

G.M. gave out the first contract in 1953. It was for the glass body. It went to a company in Ohio. The deal cost $4,000,000. There were 12,000 cars made. Each one weighed close to 400 pounds. That weight was less than if the cars had been made of steel. The Vette body was light. That meant more speed. The first cars were made by hand. Three of them were made each day. From that time on, the Corvette would raise eyebrows.

*This is the famous crossed flags insignia
of the Corvette.*

CHAPTER 2

THE VETTE BECOMES A LEGEND

The Corvette was now on the road. G.M. was proud. They had built their sports car, and it was a fine one. The Vette was made for America. It was fast and it was pretty. The price was perfect. Earl had kept his promise. Yes, the Vette was on the road, but the story was far from over. The car had leaks. It made too much noise. It sometimes rolled on turns. If the Vette was here to stay, it would need some help.

The man of the hour was Z.A. Duntov. From the time he first saw it, he knew that the Vette would need changes. It was Duntov who would help make the changes and save the Vette many times. Duntov was like the Vette. He was elegant. He was tough. He took chances, and he came through. He had come through twice before in his life. He came through World War II, and he came from a unique home life. His father and stepfather both lived with his mother. Duntov felt it was a happy home, but just not the same as others. You may think this is a strange story for a top man in the car world. Yet, Duntov is called "Mr. Corvette."

Duntov first saw the Vette at a show. It was the "motorama." He thought the car looked great, the best car he had seen. But, he knew it had problems. He knew it had to improve. He wrote a letter to G.M. Ed Cole, a top man there, read it. In the letter was a new plan for the Vette. Cole, who owned a Vette, knew the car needed help. Once he had driven his Vette from Detroit to Kalamazoo in the rain. The water flowed into the Vette. Cole had to take his shoes and socks off. He drove without shoes all the way. Then he lost his camera in the flood. Ed decided to give Duntov the job of saving the Vette.

The first thing Duntov did was to test the car. It steered too wide up front. It steered too short in the back. He fixed that. The Vette could now make it out of a drift. Fumes were the next test. A driver had to breathe them in. Duntov had to find a better place to put the tail pipes. They were put in the rear bumper. This new improvement helped.

Duntov designed a fuel injection system. This was another Vette first! He also improved the cam. This gave the Vette a fast start and a quick stop. Almost the whole car was to change. It was once more a great car. Sales picked up. A new Vette was born and it was burning rubber!

In 1956 the car plant that made the Corvettes was moved. The new plant was large and clean. G.M. wanted to make the Vette a real success.

This is the Corvette engine with the fuel injection system that Duntov designed.

In 1958 the Vette had a new design drawn by Billy Mitchell. Here you can see the rear end styling and the parking lights placed below the bumper guard.

CHAPTER 3

THE ERA OF THE STING RAY

In 1958 there was a big change. The Vette had a new design. Billy Mitchell drew it. The new Vette had a great look. It was tested. It was raced. It was improved. It was a work of art. Its name was the Sting Ray. It had grace. It had a clean line. And it was fast. The fuel injection system was refined. That had not been done since the year it was first put in. The Corvette coupe could go up to 160 miles per hour. The roadster model was a bit slower. The team that made this Vette was proud. For the fans, it was true love! Sales grew. Of 10,000 cars that sold, half were coupes and half were convertibles. The Vette came of age. The market was big. The dream car looked great. It was fast. The price was right. These were the Vette trademarks.

*The 1963 Corvette Sting Ray Sport
Coupe had head lamps that could open
and close.*

The Sting Ray was made of fiberglass. Twin
tail pipes ran down the sides. Its rear was smooth
and sleek. On the road, it was great. *Motor Trend*
magazine gave it a 10 rating. But it got poor
grades, too! The dials on the dashboard were in
the wrong place. The steering wheel was too
high. It made too much noise. It was hard for
the driver to see the road.

CHAPTER 4

MAKO SHARK II

By 1965 the race was on. Now Ford Motor Company and other car makers had dream cars, too. G.M. needed a Vette that could compete with the new cars. G.M. would forge a new dream. They would make a new Vette. It would be a car for now and a car for the future. It would be a car that could last. G.M. wanted a car that could beat Ford. That car was the Mako Shark II.

The first Mako was the X-15. It was not seen by the fans. It did serve as a model. It does not exist now, but all Vettes have a piece of it in their designs.

The frame was the same as the one used on the Sting Ray. It was lower and longer. The Mako Shark II had four-wheel disc brakes. It had a low hood. It was lean. It was tough! The Mako shape was all power.

The Mako had high fenders and a fast back. The back had six slots. This cut down on wind drag. You could take off the whole top.

The Vette changed in 1969. That year it was named Sting ray. The word ray was written with a small "r." It was to be a fancy Vette. It was not as fast or as smooth as the other models. Most of the cars would be coupes.

The new cars had more room. The cockpit was safe. Lights would warn of loose doors. There were seatbelts. There were three-speed gears and four-speed gears. There was turbo drive. That year the engine was new. It was made of aluminum. It weighed 100 pounds less than the old engine that was made of iron.

The cost of the new engine was high. It cost $3,000 more than the old one. The 1969 model had problems, too. Some new items failed. The head lamps did not always close. They made noise. It was a fair year for sales. The crew of Apollo 12 each had a new Vette. Pete Conrad, Dick Gordon and Al Bean all had been to the moon. They all drove their Vettes with pride.

That year a Vette won a big race at Daytona. Jerry Thompson drove the winning car. It was named the Champ, "The Production Car of the Year." This was the first win since 1962. It was a push for Vette makers. It was a joy for Vette fans. The dream was still on the road.

CHAPTER 5

THE ALL-AROUND-TOWN VETTE

In 1970, a new Vette was made. It looked like the Mako II. It acted like the Sting ray. Its name was the Aero-Coupe. The biggest change in this new car was in the cockpit. Looks came first. The way the car drove came second. There were leather trimmed seats and deep pile rugs. These luxuries were now popular. The car had wood-grain trim on the dash and doors made to look expensive. The Aero-Coupe had the most up-to-date rear end and a four-speed gear box. All this came with each new Vette. It was a hit.

The Vette reached a high peak that year. It was thought to be the best car in appearance and the best car for the road.

The Vette top brass asked for more. They wanted the Vette to be better. More hard work had to be done. New ways had to be found. This meant a higher price tag. Yet that year Vettes were sold out. This began a new trend. Each year

In 1970 the new Sting ray was made.

all Vettes sold very well. Some were even sold in advance. There was a waiting list. This trend still goes on today. If you want a new Vette, you must wait. But the wait is not long, a few months, at the most. And it's worth it. It must be, because each year the list grows.

The Aero-Coupe also had a new engine. The engine was called the LT-1. It was quick and light. Its time was quick, from 0 to 102 mph in 14.2 seconds. This was the hottest quarter mile ever for the Vette. Duntov was proud and so was the whole G.M. team. The Vette fans bought every Aero-Coupe made.

CHAPTER 6

A TOUGH TEST FOR THE VETTE

It was now 1971. The world had a new problem. So did the Vette. The price of gas went up. G.M. had to help. They cut the octane use in all their cars. The new goal was to save fuel and clean up the air. The Vette was part of the new plan. The octane used by the Vette was changed from 103 to 91. This meant less horsepower. The era of the big engine was gone. The fancy car was on its way out, too.

Clean air standards were set. Fans wanted to use less fuel. The new Vette engine was small. It was almost the size of the first Vette engine. That year 10,000 Vettes were sold. This meant the work could go slowly. G.M. could take more time. Each part could be put in with care. The Vette was built better. It was now a quality car. The team at G.M. was proud. It was a good feeling. The pride was shared by the Vette fans. They smiled more.

The 1973 Sting ray kept some of the old Vette designs, but it had many new features.

The new Vettes were tested in many ways. There was a test for leaks. Each car had a four-minute wash, like a shower. All the leaks were fixed. There was also a test for noise. Each car was raced for two miles. The track was tough. If noise was found, it was fixed.

Two Vettes were carved out of the pack. They were not for the street. They were to race. One was the ZR-1. The other was the ZR-2. The ZR-2 had a Mark IV engine. Duntov said these cars were not for the road. They were too fast. They were not smooth. They were too noisy.

Some fans did not care. They wanted them for street use. They got their wish.

By 1972 the radial-ply tire came out. These tires were new to the racing world. The Vette used them. The Vette had a great year in 1972. It won a few races. One reason for its success was the new tires. They were fast. They were safe. They were a good choice for the Vette. It was Duntov who decided to use them. The radial-ply tire was safe at top speeds. In 1973 they were put in general use. All the stock Vettes had them. They were the best tires on the market.

That same year the range of horsepower fell. The spread of speed was from 190 to 275 mph. Some parts of the car had to be retooled. The cost was high, almost too high. The Vette was almost scrapped. But that year it was to pass a most important test. It was a true victory for G.M. For the Vette, it was one more chance.

A new body mount was made for the Corvette. It reduced the noise. It had a smooth ride.

It was made of rubber with a steel insert. It could stop the drum noise of the body. A new paint was used. It was an asphalt mix. This made the body shake less. The Vette could ride on rough roads without making so much noise.

That year the Vette raced down south. It won at Daytona. It was, after all, a great machine.

In that same year, 30,000 cars were sold. The fans wanted more. There were not enough Vettes made. The next year, 34,000 cars were made. The year after, 38,000 cars were made.

The cost of the Corvette was $6,000. The Vette had more fans than ever! Money was no object. Fans loved the Vette.

CHAPTER 7

THE END OF AN ERA (1975)

Change came to the world of cars. The Vette had to change, too. There were new rules about clean air and about fuel. The size of motors had to change. They had to be small and they had to use less gas. The engines had to burn cleanly. Chevy let go of the big Mark IV. A new engine, the L-48, was used. It had less power and used no-lead gas. Another change took place. Duntov retired. The Vette's best friend was gone. The Corvette was his dream, his risk, his car. And, it was his success. The Vette was now on its own. So was Duntov. Both would make it in the years ahead.

Duntov's helper took the wheel. Dave McLellan was the new boss, the new man of the hour. He knew the Vette well. He knew where it came from. He knew where it could go. But it was not an easy change. The convertible Vette was no longer made. The coupe was safer. It was dry

The 1975 Corvette had improved performance and an elegant design.

and it was warm. The fans wanted a convertible, but they would have to live without one. Their dream had to change a bit. The old dream was a convertible, a fast car, at a fair price. That *was* the first Vette dream. The new dream was a fast coupe that was safe. It was also clean but not cheap! It fit new rules. It fit a new dream.

In this new era, change came slowly. Changes were made to a curve here, a line there. But, there were no great sweeps. Why make a new Vette? This one was doing fine. All of them did well. Each year they were all sold. The fans loved it. Research was not done to change the style, but to improve safety features. A new dream car would come later.

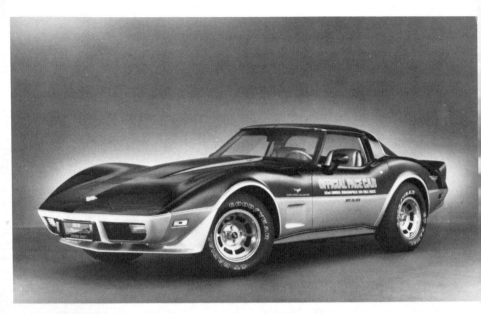

*The 1978 Indianapolis 500 pace car was
this Special Edition Corvette.*

CHAPTER 8

THE MID-ENGINE VETTE

The first Vette was made from a dream. The car was all about dreams. Ideas found their way into test cars. New parts were used. If they did well, great. If not, then they came out. To make a new car is hard. Parts have to be made. Some have to be found. They are often found in other cars, cars that are already on the road. This was true for the XP 800, the mid-engine Vette. Most of its parts came from other Vettes. Some parts were made in research labs. The gearbox came from another car, the Tempest. It was the best, so it was used. The brakes came from the Vette that was already on the road.

The rack and pinion steering was made by hand. The whole car was sleek. It was a mid-engine dream car and it was on a real track. G.M. had great hope for it. The mid-sized cars did well at the race tracks. They were loved by the race fans. The car makers thought well of them. The Ford Motor Company had a mid-sized racer, too. Other car makers did, too. The XP drove for 1,000 miles. It was good, but it was not great. The Vette team had to work harder. It had a long way to go. In the end it might win.

CHAPTER 9

THE ONCE AND FUTURE VETTE

In 1980, the Vette was still here. It was one of the best sports cars. It was a fast two-seater at a good price. It was clean and fuel-efficient. The dream was still strong. As McLellan said, "We test the Vette for what it has to do. Can it do what it should do? How well can it perform?" Car fans thought the Vette was the best, in its class or out of it. News reports said the same thing. The Vette is here to stay.

The new Vette had grown. It had a fiberglass rear spring. It was strong. It had a four-speed shift. The four on the floor was back!

The 1980 Vette was one of the best sports cars. It was a fast two-seater at a good price.

*This 1981 Corvette had a fiberglass
rear spring and a four-speed shift.*

The Vette had a new part, a brain! This brain
was a computer that would save gas. It was called
the CCC system (Command Control). The Vette
had a quartz clock and a clear AM and FM radio.
The car was smooth. It was elegant. It was a
dream for the 1980s. They all sold. The fans
wanted more. They wanted a dream for the future. The Vette would be it!

A new factory was built. It was a new place
to work and to build a dream car. It was in Kentucky. There, G.M. built a new Vette. It was an
original, the first original in many years.

*The world has changed much since 1952,
and so has the Vette. The 1983
Corvette is a new classic in an old mold.*

CHAPTER 10

STATE OF THE ART

This is the story of the Corvette and how it came to be. The story goes on. It is like a great scenic road. It leads from the past to the future. It leads out of a secret room at G.M. It goes all the way to the world's center stage. The Vette grew from a dream car to a high-tech masterpiece.

The year is now! The world has changed much since the first Vette. So has G.M. It is a new era. Dave McAllen, once under Duntov, is now the boss. His soft spot is still the dream car. The Vette will live on, but it will be brand new. It will be a new classic in an old mold.

Jerry Palmer, of the G.M. design staff, drew it. "I think," he says, "we have made a whole new car. But, it still is a Vette. It still has a Vette face. But, now there are fog lamps where there were air vents. The old rear spoiler is still in use." Palmer goes on to say, "When fans see the new

*Take a close look at the
1983 Vette's chassis.*

Vette, they will know it. But when they see it next to a 1982, wow! They will see a real change."

The new Vette was born out of the mid-engine group. The mid-engine style was not a good choice for G.M., but that style was perfect for a start. From there the new Vette was tested on the drawing board. It was tested in a wind tunnel. It was tested on the track. It took years and years to style. The end result was a brand new Vette, a car of and for this new era.

The new hood is shaped like a clam shell. Under it, the hardware is very neat. It sports a crossfire fuel injection system. This is a big step ahead of Duntov's first injection system.

A new type of air cleaner is used. It has a belt drive with a snake-like look and an electric fan. Even the oil dipstick has a T-shape. All the parts look and work as one unit. Even the Delco battery is black and gray to match the engine.

This Vette has a V-8 engine. It has 205 horsepower. It comes with a four-speed automatic gearbox. Some Vettes may have a four-speed manual transmission. It comes with a computer set for overdrive.

In the cockpit the dials are easy to see. Most can be read at a glance. Most have back-up lights. The controls are made with real leather. The seats look and feel great. They were made to look and feel that way for many years.

On the road, the Vette has taken a big step, too. It is tight on turns and quick on the getaway. It is smooth at all speeds. The new car is light in weight. Its body is made in one piece. The

The new Corvette is a world class car.

*In the cockpit of the 1983 Corvette
the dials are easy to read.*

frame is strong. It uses new metal alloys for the first time. Aluminum parts make the Vette light and strong. The tires are the most up-to-date wide aspect from Goodyear. Each wheel is made for the right or left side of the Vette. All in all, it is a world class car, a state of the art machine.

The new Vette is said to be the best road Vette ever. *Motor Trend* magazine calls it the best at any price. By the way, the price is not cheap. The new Vette costs more than $20,000. But, for the price, the Vette is an excellent value. From all points of view, the Vette is a world class car.

It can compete with the Porsche 928. It can hold its own with the Ferrari. And it can stay with the Maserati all the way down the track!

McAllen says, "To find a peer to the Vette you have to look very far.There are other cars made in small amounts, but at two or three times the price of our Vette." Quality is just part of the new Vette story. The Vette is also a dream car. It has comfort and beauty as well.

The Vette seems to be a winner. It has passed its tests, the tests at the race tracks and the tests at G.M. It has also passed the test of love from its fans. It is a dream car that is here to stay.

CHAPTER 11

NEW HOME FOR THE VETTE

The newest Vette plant is in Bowling Green, Kentucky. It is the third home of the Vette. The first home was in Flint, Michigan. The first 300 cars were made there. The second home was in St. Louis. It stayed there for three decades!

In June of 1981, the new plant opened. It turned out its first new Vette. G.M. now had an all-sports-car plant. The all new Vette came out that year.

Computers are a part of the new plant. They work on the assembly line. There, nuts and bolts are made tight. Welds are made. This work has to be done for each Vette. Great care is needed. The auto-tool does it all. It keeps a record of each job done.

Each day the Vette line team meets for a chat. They talk about the Vette. They talk about each Vette as it is made. They discuss how it can be made better. They view each car, one at a

The workers at the Bowling Green Plant
are proud of their work.

time, not as a long line of tasks. They are proud of their work. They make sure each Vette is a great one.

This year the Vette will be sold outside of the U.S.A., too. It will be sold in Europe and Japan. G.M. thinks it will do well there. Says R.C. Stempel, a vice president at G.M., "The world will see what the Vette is all about." The Vette may soon be the dream car of the world.

1984 CORVETTE SPECIFICATIONS

Two-door Hatchback Coupe (two passenger)

Engine:	5.7-liter V8 (350 cu. in.) 205 hp at 4300 rpm Cast iron alloy block Aluminum alloy pistons Cast alloy iron camshaft Bore: 4.00; Stroke: 3.48
Engine Weight:	584 pounds
Transmissions:	Four-speed manual with computer-controlled overdrive in 2nd, 3rd, and 4th gears
	Four-speed automatic (overdrive)
Fuel:	Unleaded 20-gallon capacity tank Fuel injection, electronic control, pulse action
Tires:	Steel-belted radial. 35 lb. psi

Wheels:	8.5″ front, 9.5″ rear, cast aluminum
Brakes:	Four-wheel disc
Steering:	Power, rack and pinion Tilt and telescopic steering wheel
Suspension:	Front: SLA design with fiberglass leaf spring
	Rear: Five-link fully independent
Body:	All-welded body-frame with bolt-on front to allow bottom load of engine
Width:	71.0 inches
Length:	176.5 inches
Height:	46.9 inches
Curb Weight:	3,192 pounds

This experimental "idea" car was called
the Corvette Mulsanne. It was developed
by the G.M. design staff.

WHO BUYS CHEVROLET'S CORVETTE
IN THE U.S.A?

Age — 72 percent of the Vette buyers are between 25 and 44 years of age (specifically, 38 percent are 25-34 and 34 percent are 35-44). Only four percent are over 55 while 11 percent are under 25.

Education — 40 percent are college graduates. 80 percent have had some college or technical school training. Only one percent failed to achieve at least a high school diploma.

Occupation — 71 percent are white collar workers and another 17 percent are blue collar workers.

Marital Status — 59 percent of Corvette purchasers are married.

A
Corvette
GALLERY

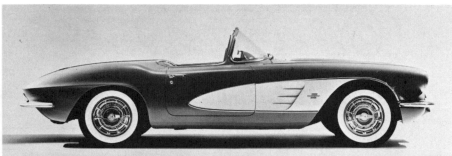

*Here are three views of the classic 1961
Corvette.*

The 1962 Vette on the road.

*Here are three views of the 1963 Corvette
Sting Ray convertible.*

This 1963 Corvette Sting Ray Sport
Coupe has a steel framework that sur-
rounds the passenger area for less noise
and greater safety.

*Here is another view of the 1963 Corvette
Sting Ray Sport Coupe.*

*The 1967 Corvette had new emblems
and ornamentation.*

*These three experimental or "idea"
Corvettes were developed in the late
sixties and early seventies.*

FURTHER READING

Julty, Sam. *How Your Car Works.* Harper and Row, New York, 1974.

Packard, Chris. *Safe Driving.* J.B. Lippincott Company, New York, 1974.

Wailtey, Douglas. *The Roads We Traveled.* Julian Messner, New York, 1979.

Weissler, Paul. *Basic Car Maintenance.* Harper and Row, New York, 1981.

INDEX

ABOUT THE AUTHOR

Jeffrey Hoffman lives and writes in New York City. He has written articles and books on such subjects as microcomputers and space travel. This is his fourth book for young adults.